★ **It's My State!** ★ ★ ★ ★

# WEST VIRGINIA

## The Mountain State

Rick Petreycik and Gerry Boehme

Cavendish Square

New York

Published in 2017 by Cavendish Square Publishing, LLC
243 5th Avenue, Suite 136, New York, NY 10016

Copyright © 2017 by Cavendish Square Publishing, LLC

Third Edition

Website: cavendishsq.com

This publication represents the opinions and views of the author based on his or her personal experience, knowledge, and research. The information in this book serves as a general guide only. The author and publisher have used their best efforts in preparing this book and disclaim liability rising directly or indirectly from the use and application of this book.

CPSIA Compliance Information: Batch #CS16CSQ

All websites were available and accurate when this book was sent to press.

Library of Congress Cataloging-in-Publication Data

Names: Petreycik, Rick, author. | Boehme, Gerry, author.
Title: West Virginia / Rick Petreycik and Gerry Boehme.
Description: Third edition. | New York : Cavendish Square Publishing, 2016. |
Series: It's my state! | Includes index. | Description based on print
version record and CIP data provided by publisher; resource not viewed.
Identifiers: LCCN 2015046175 (print) | LCCN 2015045737 (ebook) | ISBN
9781627132589 (ebook) | ISBN 9781627132565 (library bound)
Subjects: LCSH: West Virginia--Juvenile literature.
Classification: LCC F241.3 (print) | LCC F241.3 .P47 2016 (ebook) | DDC
975.4--dc23
LC record available at http://lccn.loc.gov/2015046175

Editorial Director: David McNamara
Editor: Fletcher Doyle
Copy Editor: Nathan Heidelberger
Art Director: Jeffrey Talbot
Designer: Joseph Macri
Production Assistant: Karol Szymczuk
Photo Research: J8 Media

# WEST VIRGINIA

## CONTENTS

## ★ State Animal: Black Bear

These medium-sized bears live mostly in West Virginia's eastern mountain region. Black bears usually have black or dark brown fur. They have rounded ears, small eyes, and five strong claws on each paw. Their strong sense of smell helps them find their favorite foods, including nuts, berries, fruits, acorns, and roots.

## ★ State Bird: Cardinal

The male cardinal is bright red with a black throat. The female is sandy brown and black with patches of red on its wings, tail, and crest. These birds measure about 8 inches (20.3 centimeters) and are known for their distinctive sounds, singing nearly all year long.

## ★ State Fish: Trout

The brook trout is the only trout species, or type, that is native to West Virginia. Brook trout thrive in the state's many pure, cool mountain streams. Brook trout are usually green or dark brown and can grow to be nearly 10 inches (25.4 cm) in length.

# WEST VIRGINIA

## POPULATION: 1,852,994

## ★ State Flower: Rhododendron

Governor George Atkinson, who first suggested the state choose an official flower, once said, "I know none more beautiful and none more common in West Virginia than the rhododendron. It is found along most every vale and hillside and is universally admired for both its beauty and fragrance."

## ★ State Fruit: Golden Delicious Apple

The apple had been West Virginia's official fruit until 1995, when the state specifically selected the golden delicious apple, first discovered in Clay County in 1905. Each year, the county holds the Clay County Golden Delicious Festival to celebrate the popular fruit with a parade, pageants, and a baking contest.

## ★ State Tree: Sugar Maple

The tall sugar maple, which sometimes reaches a height of 80 feet (24 meters), is valued for its beautiful foliage, its hard wood, and its sweet sap, which is used to make maple syrup. The tree's lumber is used to make furniture and musical instruments, such as guitars and pianos.

Running water from the state's many rivers and streams powered mills and provided transportation routes in West Virginia.

# The Mountain State

"Oh, the West Virginia hills! How majestic and how grand,
With their summits bathed in glory, Like our Prince Immanuel's Land!
Is it any wonder then, That my heart with rapture thrills,
As I stand once more with loved ones On those West Virginia hills?"

When Ellen King wrote the lyrics to her song "West Virginia Hills" back in 1885, she may not have realized at the time how she had captured the feelings of residents and visitors alike, all of whom are struck by the majestic mountains and tremendous beauty of this remarkable state. In fact, she did her job so well that the West Virginia Legislature selected "West Virginia Hills" as the state's first official song in 1947.

The words that Ellen King wrote back then still ring true today. While relatively small compared to other states, West Virginia boasts a wealth of scenery, wildlife, and natural resources, and its fascinating history provides a unique perspective on how America has grown and adapted to change over the years.

West Virginia is located in the southeastern portion of the United States. With a total land area of 24,038 square miles (62,258 square kilometers), it ranks forty-first in size among the fifty states. From north to south, West Virginia measures about 236 miles (380 kilometers). From east to west it is close to 264 miles (425 km).

The Allegheny Mountains run for about 400 miles (644 km) through West Virginia.

## Strange Shape

If you look at a map of West Virginia, you will see that its shape is unusual. To some, it almost looks like a frog with its two hind legs spread out. The "hind legs" are the two narrow strips of land called panhandles. The Northern Panhandle lies between Ohio and Pennsylvania, while the Eastern Panhandle cuts between Maryland and Virginia.

Much of West Virginia's land is mountainous. In fact, with an average height of 1,500 feet (457 m), West Virginia has the highest elevation of any state east of the Mississippi River. For that reason, it has been nicknamed the Mountain State. Some geographers believe that if West Virginia's mountainous regions were flattened out, the area covered would extend well beyond the borders of the entire United States.

The state's mountains are the result of events that shaped the landscape around 245 million years ago. During a mountain-building era known as the Appalachian Orogeny, a great inland sea covered much of the interior of North America, and great pressure drove a portion of the floor upward to create the Appalachian Mountains. Over millions

| West Virginia Borders | |
|---|---|
| North: | Pennsylvania Maryland Ohio |
| South: | Virginia |
| East: | Virginia |
| West: | Kentucky Ohio |

of years, the new land was worn down by wind and rain and became a large plain, tilting gently toward the Mississippi valley. Natural forces, including erosion and the flow of streams, eventually produced a terrain marked by the numerous valleys, rugged hills, and mountains that distinguish the state's landscape to this day.

That period also began the formation of the immense deposits of coal, oil, natural gas, salt, limestone, and other resources that have proved vital to the economic life of West Virginia. The huge glaciers of the Ice Age never reached present-day West Virginia, but they did play a major role in forming the state's flowing rivers and streams.

Mountains separate West Virginia's three main land regions. The Appalachian Ridge and Valley region is located east of the Allegheny Mountains. The Allegheny Mountains begin in central Pennsylvania and extend through West Virginia and Maryland. West Virginia's portion of the Allegheny Mountains runs along the state's eastern border with Virginia. These are the tallest mountains in the state. West Virginia's highest point, Spruce Knob, is located among these mountains and rises more than 4,861 feet (1,482 m) above sea level.

The Appalachian Plateau region is located west of the Allegheny Mountains. This region covers about 60 percent of West Virginia's total land area. It is also the state's most densely populated region. This means that there are many people in each measured unit of land. Among the major cities located there are Wheeling, Weirton, and Charleston, the state's capital.

Historic Harpers Ferry rests between the Potomac and the Shenandoah Rivers.

# WEST VIRGINIA

## COUNTY MAP

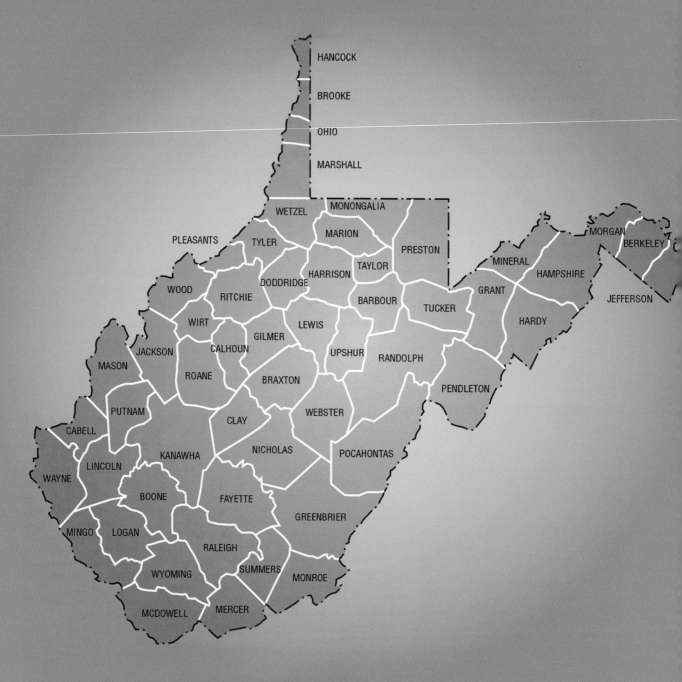

HANCOCK

BROOKE

OHIO

MARSHALL

WETZEL

MONONGALIA

PLEASANTS

TYLER

MARION

PRESTON

MORGAN

BERKELEY

WOOD

DODDRIDGE

HARRISON

TAYLOR

MINERAL

HAMPSHIRE

RITCHIE

BARBOUR

TUCKER

GRANT

JEFFERSON

WIRT

LEWIS

HARDY

JACKSON

CALHOUN

GILMER

UPSHUR

RANDOLPH

MASON

ROANE

BRAXTON

PUTNAM

WEBSTER

PENDLETON

CABELL

CLAY

KANAWHA

NICHOLAS

POCAHONTAS

WAYNE

LINCOLN

BOONE

FAYETTE

GREENBRIER

MINGO

LOGAN

RALEIGH

SUMMERS

MONROE

WYOMING

MCDOWELL

MERCER

# WEST VIRGINIA

## POPULATION BY COUNTY

| County | Population | County | Population | County | Population |
|--------|-----------:|--------|-----------:|--------|-----------:|
| Barbour | 16,589 | Marshall | 33,107 | Webster | 9,154 |
| Berkeley | 104,169 | Mason | 27,324 | Wetzel | 16,583 |
| Boone | 24,629 | Mercer | 62,264 | Wirt | 5,717 |
| Braxton | 14,523 | Mineral | 28,212 | Wood | 86,956 |
| Brooke | 24,069 | Mingo | 26,839 | Wyoming | 23,796 |
| Cabell | 96,319 | Monongalia | 96,189 | | |
| Calhoun | 7,627 | Monroe | 13,502 | | |
| Clay | 9,386 | Morgan | 17,541 | | |
| Doddridge | 8,202 | Nicholas | 26,233 | | |
| Fayette | 46,039 | Ohio | 44,443 | | |
| Gilmer | 8,693 | Pendleton | 7,695 | | |
| Grant | 11,937 | Pleasants | 7,605 | | |
| Greenbrier | 35,480 | Pocahontas | 8,719 | | |
| Hampshire | 23,964 | Preston | 33,520 | | |
| Hancock | 30,676 | Putnam | 55,486 | | |
| Hardy | 14,025 | Raleigh | 78,859 | | |
| Harrison | 69,099 | Randolph | 29,405 | | |
| Jackson | 29,211 | Ritchie | 10,449 | | |
| Jefferson | 53,498 | Roane | 14,926 | | |
| Kanawha | 193,063 | Summers | 13,927 | | |
| Lewis | 16,372 | Taylor | 16,895 | | |
| Lincoln | 21,720 | Tucker | 7,141 | | |
| Logan | 36,743 | Tyler | 9,208 | | |
| McDowell | 22,113 | Upshur | 24,254 | | |
| Marion | 56,418 | Wayne | 42,481 | | |

Source: U.S. Bureau of the Census, 2010

Waterfalls are common in West Virginia as rivers flow out of the mountains.

The third West Virginia region includes the Blue Ridge Mountains. This range is located at the eastern tip of West Virginia's Eastern Panhandle. The mountains are part of the Appalachian Mountain chain that extends from Maine all the way down to Alabama. The Shenandoah Mountains are located in this region.

The Shenandoah River flows through West Virginia's Blue Ridge region. The river has deposited rich soil that supports the state's thriving peach and apple orchards. Martinsburg, the state's center of commerce and recreation, is located in this area. Another West Virginia river is the Potomac, which passes alongside Harpers Ferry—a scenic Blue Ridge town that played a major role in the country's history.

## Waterways

While West Virginia is primarily known as "The Mountain State," it could just as easily have been called "The River State." With eleven of its rivers equipped with locks and dams at some point in the state's history, West Virginia holds the distinction of having had more locks and dams than any other state in the nation.

The rivers and streams of eight Eastern Panhandle counties flow into the Potomac River, which marks the border between West Virginia and Maryland. The rivers and streams of the remaining forty-seven counties find their way into the Ohio River as it flows along the state's western boundary for 277 miles (446 km), more than a fourth of the river's total length. For these 277 miles, the Ohio River is included within the territory of West Virginia, with the state line running along the opposite shore.

The New River Gorge becomes lined with color when cooler weather arrives in the fall.

Superstorm Sandy brought heavy snow to West Virginia in 2012, toppling trees onto power lines.

Besides the Shenandoah, Ohio, and Potomac, there are other major rivers in the state. These include the Kanawha, Elk, Coal, Pocatalico, Little Kanawha, Guyandotte, Tug Fork, Big Sandy, Monongahela, Cheat, Tygart, West Fork, Back Creek, Cacapon, New, and Greenbrier Rivers. Rivers form several boundary lines between West Virginia and neighboring states. The Ohio River separates West Virginia from the state of Ohio. The Tug Fork and Big Sandy Rivers define the state's borders with both Virginia and Kentucky. In the north, the Potomac River flows along West Virginia's border with Maryland.

West Virginia also has about seventy small lakes and ponds. All of them are man-made. Many of them were formed when dams were built across rivers and other waterways. These dams help control melted snow, rainwater, and overflow from West Virginia's many rivers and streams. The state's largest reservoirs, or man-made lakes, are Summersville Lake and Sutton Lake. Both are located in the central part of the state.

## Climate

West Virginia has cold winters and hot summers. However, different regions in the state vary in average temperatures. For example, residents living in the low-lying Appalachian Plateau may have summer temperatures around 87 degrees Fahrenheit (30.5 degrees Celsius). Average temperatures in mountain towns, however, are a little cooler, at around 82°F (27.7°C).

# 10 KEY SITES ★ ★ ★

### 1. Blackwater Falls State Park

This park is named for the falls of the Blackwater River, which plunge five stories, then twist and tumble through an 8-mile (13 km) **gorge**. The "black" water is colored by **tannic acid** from fallen hemlock and red spruce needles.

Blackwater Falls State Park

### 2. Cass Scenic Railroad

Nestled in the mountains, the Cass Scenic Railroad travels the same line built in 1901 to haul lumber to the mill in Cass. Vintage Shay steam locomotives were designed to climb the steepest grades and swing around hairpin curves.

Cass Scenic Railroad

### 3. Charleston Civic Center

With the capacity to seat more than thirteen thousand guests, the Charleston Civic Center hosts concerts by national artists, athletic events, and shows like *Disney On Ice*, as well as fairs, festivals, and expos.

### 4. Harpers Ferry

At Harpers Ferry, visitors can step back in time as living history exhibits offer the opportunity to meet Civil War–era characters. Among the attractions is the John Brown Wax Museum, where you can discover more about the town's history.

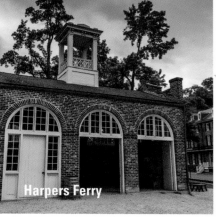

Harpers Ferry

### 5. Midland Trail

The Midland Trail National Scenic Byway takes drivers off the interstate. The road winds and rolls 180 miles (290 km) across West Virginia's midsection. Travel border to border and see mountain lakes, streams, waterfalls, fields, and big cities.

# WEST VIRGINIA

### 6. Monongahela National Forest

Located in the north-central highlands of West Virginia, the Monongahela straddles the highest ridges in the state. Its varying precipitation and terrain make the Monongahela National Forest one of the most **ecologically diverse** forests in the country.

### 7. New River Gorge Bridge

Among the oldest rivers on the continent, the whitewaters of New River flow amid sloping mountains. Be sure to take the Bridge Walk Tour, where you can see breathtaking scenery as you walk at a leisurely pace along the bridge.

### 8. Seneca Caverns

Seneca Caverns were born 460 million years ago when the cavern's limestone bed first formed. Named for the Seneca Native Americans who used them for shelter and storage, they stretch 165 feet (50 m) below the entrance.

### 9. State Capitol

West Virginia's most recognizable building, the Charleston State Capitol, is best known for its 293-foot (89 m) golden dome, 5 feet (1.5 m) higher than the US Capitol's dome. Builders used more than seven hundred train carloads of limestone and 4,500 tons (4,082 metric tons) of steel.

### 10. West Virginia State Museum

Visitors can tour the West Virginia State Museum in Charleston to learn about the state's culture, art, **paleontology**, archaeology, and geology. This museum showcases a collection that began in 1890.

Monongahela National Forest

New River Gorge Bridge

State Capitol

In January, the average low temperature in West Virginia's mountainous areas is 22°F (–5.5°C). In the state's southernmost region, the average January low is 27°F (–2.7°C). Even though the thermometers in West Virginia can hit below the freezing mark, or 32°F (0°C), it is very unusual for winter temperatures to stay below freezing for more than a couple of days.

West Virginia's Eastern Panhandle, which is not too far from the Atlantic Ocean, experiences moderate coastal weather conditions throughout most of the year. Winds blowing in from the Atlantic Ocean help cool the air in summer. These winds also keep the temperatures from getting too cold in the winter. West Virginia, however, occasionally experiences extreme weather conditions. The temperature soared to a sizzling 112°F (44.4°C) at Moorfield on August 4, 1930, and at Martinsburg on July 10, 1936. At the other extreme, the temperature fell to a bone-numbing –37°F (–38.3°C) at Lewisburg on December 30, 1917.

West Virginia gets plenty of precipitation each year. Around 44 inches (112 cm) of water falls on the state as rain, sleet, or snow. Yearly snowfall varies throughout the state. It ranges from an average of 20 inches (51 cm) in the southwest to nearly 100 inches (254 cm) in the mountainous areas. Very little snow falls in the coastal Eastern Panhandle area.

## River Staircase

Ships and barges use systems called locks to "step" up or down a river or canal from one water level to another. Locks are big chambers in the water with moveable gates at each end. Water is pumped in and out of the lock to raise or lower the boat.

The Dolly Sods Wilderness rewards hikers with beautiful views.

At times, West Virginia can have too much precipitation. Flooding near the state's river valleys can be dangerous. In the past, overflowing rivers have destroyed entire West Virginia towns.

Due to the nature of its terrain, West Virginia also happens to be one of the more cloudy areas of the country. Beckley, Elkins, and Huntington all average about two hundred days per year with overcast conditions. These locations are among the cloudiest in the eastern United States. Fog is the biggest culprit for causing these cloudy conditions.

West Virginia's famous fog comes from two main sources: trees and mountains. Much of the state is covered by trees and plants, which are responsible for putting a lot of moisture into the air through something called transpiration. Transpiration is the process in which trees and plants absorb water from the ground through their roots and then give off water vapor through pores in their leaves. Then, since West Virginia is so mountainous, much of the state cools quickly after the sun goes down due to the high elevation. This produces cold air that drops down into the valleys. When the cold air hits the water vapor still floating in the air, the combination produces thick clouds of fog. Several towns in the state report dense fog (visibilities below 0.25 miles or .4 km) for at least forty days per year.

## Wildlife

West Virginia is home to a variety of plants and animals. The forests in West Virginia are especially important to the state's wildlife. About three hundred years ago, the area that would become West Virginia was covered with thick forests. Over the years, forest fires and logging by humans reduced the number of trees in the region. Today, however, second-growth trees, trees that have grown after the original forest was cut down, and later-growth trees are plentiful everywhere. In fact, they now cover about 78 percent of the state's total land area.

Among the trees that are found in West Virginia forests are softwoods such as spruce, hemlock, and white pine. Beech, hickory, sugar maple, and yellow birch

The yellow lady's slipper is one of the more than two hundred flowering plants and shrubs that grow in the Mountain State.

are also found throughout the state. Hardwoods, such as cherry and oak, thrive in West Virginia. All of these trees provide food or shelter for a number of the state's animals.

Trees are not the only plants that thrive in West Virginia. The Mountain State is also home to more than two hundred types of flowering plants and shrubs. These include sawtooth sunflowers, pitcher plants, bog rosemaries, bloodroots, goldenrods, and azaleas.

Black bears, groundhogs, rabbits, raccoons, skunks, squirrels, bobcats, and white-tailed deer are just some of the animals that live on West Virginia land. A variety of birds nest in West Virginia's trees and fly through the state's skies. These include brown thrashers, cardinals, eagles, snipes, falcons, hawks, owls, quails, and scarlet tanagers. Different species of geese, ducks, and other water birds live on or alongside the state's waterways. The waters are also filled with many different types of fish, including walleye, bass, and trout.

The last century has brought great change to West Virginia's wildlife. As human settlements grew and towns and cities developed, large amounts of wild land were lost. Some wildlife species were forced to move to other regions of the state, or out of the state completely.

Pesticides and other chemicals used by residents have also hurt West Virginia's wildlife. For example, toxic waste from the state's mines and steel mills seeped into some of the rivers. These deadly substances poisoned many of the fish in those waterways. Not only did the fish population decline, but the animals that depended on the fish for food—such as eagles and hawks—no longer had a healthy food source.

According to the West Virginia Division of Natural Resources, eleven species of animals and four species of plants found in West Virginia are listed as endangered. An endangered species is one that is

The pollution from manufacturing and mining operations in West Virginia has damaged a lot of rivers and streams.

in danger of extinction (vanishing) in all or a large part of its habitat. Its population level is so critically low, or its habitat is so degraded, that immediate action must be taken to avoid the loss of the species.

Endangered species in West Virginia include the Cheat Mountain **salamander** and the James spinymussel. Mussels live in the bottoms of streams and cannot survive if the water quality is poor. Three of the endangered animals in the state are bats, which are threatened by a dangerous fungus that first appeared in the state in 2009.

The good news is that efforts have been made to clean up contaminated water and land in the state. Tough laws and other regulations help to reduce

The people of West Virginia have worked to improve the environment in their beautiful state.

pollution from factories. The hard work of dedicated residents and legislators has also resulted in better conditions for West Virginia wildlife. Areas have been established as wildlife sanctuaries and preserves to help protect native habitats. Laws have been passed that protect certain animals from hunting or any kind of human interference. Breeding programs and other conservation efforts have also helped some animal populations to increase in the state.

Due to these and other efforts, three species in West Virginia that were once endangered—the peregrine falcon, the northern flying squirrel, and the bald eagle—have now recovered sufficiently to remove them from the endangered list. West Virginians treasure their land and work hard to preserve its natural beauty.

# ★10★KEY PLANTS AND ANIMALS

Great Horned Owl

Honeybee

Mink

## 1. Eastern Hellbender

Hellbenders are large aquatic salamanders that can reach 24 inches (61 cm) in length. They are generally brown with irregular, dark spots on the back. Hellbenders are harmless. They live in streams and emerge at night to look for food.

## 2. Great Horned Owl

The great horned owl gets its name from the tufts of feathers on its head, which look like horns. Its bright, yellow eyes help it hunt for prey, such as small rodents. Its wingspan can reach 5 feet (1.5 m).

## 3. Honeybee

The honeybee became West Virginia's official state insect in 2002. In addition to producing its flavorful honey, the honeybee **pollinates** many of the state's crops including fruits, vegetables, and grasses. Its activity produces more benefit to the state's economy than any other insect's.

## 4. Mink

A member of the weasel family, minks are dark brown and often have a white chin and a black-tipped tail. Like most weasels, the mink has a long, slender body and short legs. Minks live along rivers, streams, lakes, and ponds.

## 5. Monarch Butterfly

West Virginia's official state butterfly since 1995, the monarch is an orange and black insect that feasts on milkweed as a caterpillar, sips nectar from flowers as a butterfly, and at summer's end, migrates to Mexico.

### 6. Northern Fence Lizard

This lizard can attain a total length of up to 7 inches (17.8 cm). They are gray, brown, or tan, with a series of dark, wavy crossbands on the back. They are fast and difficult to catch, and they live on forested hillsides.

### 7. Prickly Pear

The prickly pear is a type of cactus. Instead of having leaves like many other plants, the prickly pear has flat, fleshy pads that store water. Its oblong fruit is a common food for a variety of West Virginia wildlife.

### 8. Red Fox

These small mammals are recognizable by their orange-red fur and bushy tails. The red fox eats fruits, berries, and grasses, as well as small animals such as birds, squirrels, or mice.

### 9. Sundew

Found in West Virginia's wetlands, such as bogs and marshes, the sundew is a type of carnivorous plant, which means that it eats meat. The sundew has sticky hairs. When insects land on the hairs, they get stuck and eventually die.

### 10. White-Tailed Deer

The white-tailed deer gets its name from the white coloring under its tail and on its rump. The coats of these graceful animals change with the season. They are red-brown in summer, and gray-brown in winter, to blend in with tree trunks.

Prickly Pear

Red Fox

Sundew

The old stone St. Peter's Catholic Church is located in the national park at Harpers Ferry.

# From the Beginning

I
t is believed that North America's first residents were prehistoric people who came from Asia around 30,000 BCE. They lived on a land bridge that connected Asia with North America—near present-day Siberia—before moving into the area that is now Alaska. This land bridge disappeared into the ocean when glaciers melted at the end of the last ice age. These people were the ancestors of Native Americans. As they traveled across the continent, they hunted animals, such as caribou and deer, and gathered plants to eat, such as berries and other wild fruits.

Around 3000 BCE, these natives began to settle in the region that now includes West Virginia. Instead of moving from place to place in search of food, they began to form permanent settlements. The fertile soil was used to grow food, such as beans, corn, and squash. These early settlers also created large earthen mounds. Historians believe these mounds served as important places to hold cultural activities such as religious ceremonies. Respected leaders were buried in these mounds, along with weapons and other valued items. Because of these mounds, some historians call these people the Mound Builders.

Mounds built by these cultures can be found throughout North and South America. One of the most famous burial mounds is the Grave Creek Mound in present-day

Grave Creek Mound is one of the largest examples of burial grounds made by the Mound Builders.

Moundsville, West Virginia. This is a very wide mound that is nearly 70 feet (21 m) tall. It is believed to be the largest cone-shaped burial site in North and South America.

By the end of the sixteenth century, the Mound Builders had disappeared. No one knows exactly why. It is possible that many died from illness or lack of food. The mound-building people might have moved to other regions or joined other Native groups.

## Native American Tribes

At the start of the 1600s, several different Native groups settled on the land that would eventually become West Virginia. These included the Cherokee, Shawnee, Delaware, Mingo, Seneca, Iroquois, Tuscarora, Ottawa, and Susquehannock, to name a few. Though they all traveled through the region to hunt for food, many of them also set up permanent settlements.

One such group, the Shawnee, lived in small villages that were made up of round dwellings called wigwams. Besides hunting, the Shawnee also farmed. Another group, the Delaware, also lived in small villages. These were usually near creeks, streams, and rivers. Their homes were called longhouses and were made of grass and bark.

# Europeans Arrive

In the early 1600s, English colonists began arriving on North America's Atlantic coast. One of the areas the new colonists settled included present-day Virginia. In 1669, a German geographer named John Lederer was hired to explore the areas west of the Appalachian Mountains that were claimed by the Virginia Colony. That land included present-day West Virginia. It is possible that Lederer was one of the first Europeans to set foot in the region.

In 1671, another British expedition traveled across the Appalachians. Two explorers, Thomas Batts and Robert Fallam, scouted land near the New River that is now part of southern West Virginia. Great Britain claimed the area and called it the Ohio Valley.

**Explorers survey land in the Ohio Valley, claiming it for European kings.**

This newly explored land yielded many fur-bearing animals such as minks, beavers, and foxes. The furs, or pelts, of these animals were often used to make clothing and other accessories for people in Europe and in other colonies. This fur trade encouraged more people to settle in the region.

British and French settlements in the area changed the lives of the Native Americans living there. Settlers not only took some Native American land, but agreements and trading between the two groups affected the Natives' way of life. Settlers traded guns, kettles, clothing, and other goods in exchange for furs that the Natives had collected.

Many Natives adopted the European way of life. In addition, some Native Americans used guns and other European weapons to conquer other Native groups that did not have the same weaponry.

Further exploration and settlement continued. In the 1720s, settlers from Pennsylvania moved to the region that is now part of West Virginia's Eastern Panhandle. These settlers founded the town of Mecklenburg, which was later called Shepherdstown. Located on the banks of the Potomac River, it is the state's oldest European settlement.

# The Native People

Native Americans lived in the area we now call West Virginia long before Europeans arrived. The first inhabitants of West Virginia descended from eastern Asians who crossed the Bering Strait from Siberia to Alaska approximately thirty thousand years ago. These first peoples lived as nomads, constantly moving to follow and hunt large game animals. They built more permanent settlements as they developed more reliable food supplies including small game, fish, roots, plants, and berries. West Virginia's earliest inhabitants left hundreds of mounds and other structures scattered across the landscape.

By 1600, organized tribes such as the Delaware and Shawnee had moved into present-day West Virginia. In addition, the powerful Iroquois Confederacy began exerting its influence on the region. This Confederacy was an alliance of five Iroquois-speaking nations—Mohawk, Oneida, Onondaga, Cayuga, and Seneca—formed in present-day New York in the late 1500s. In 1722, the Tuscaroras joined the Iroquois Confederacy, which became known as the Six Nations. These tribes lived in longhouses or wigwams covered in bark or animal skins, traveled by canoe on rivers, grew crops, and hunted small game.

When Europeans first explored western Virginia in the late 1600s, the Iroquois Confederacy controlled the valley but other tribes were permitted to settle there. In addition to the Shawnee and Delaware, other tribes included the Mingo, Cherokee, Tutelo, and Saponi. As settlers and miners moved into West Virginia, many Native American groups had to sign agreements, or treaties, with the US government which granted whites the right to settle on or pass through tribal territory and restricted where Native Americans could live. Eventually, most Native American rights to the land were taken away.

Unlike many other states, no federally recognized Native American tribes live in West Virginia today. The federal government forced many tribes to leave the state in the 1800s, relocating them to Oklahoma and other western states and territories. Those that remained often faced hardship and discrimination from the whites who settled the area, so they sometimes hid their Native American heritage. Descendants of the Shawnee and Cherokee still live in West Virginia, but most people from those and other tribes live in other states.

## Spotlight on the Shawnee

The original Shawnee homeland was in Ohio, Kentucky, and Indiana, but the Shawnee were far-ranging people. Shawnee villages were located as far north as New York State and as far south as Georgia.

The Shawnee lived in wigwams, which they covered in bark.

**Homes:** The Shawnee tribe lived in wigwams, or wetus—small cone-shaped houses with an arched roof made of wooden frames. They were covered with woven mats and sheets of birch bark or animal skin.

**Government:** In the past, each Shawnee village or band was governed by its own chief and tribal council. The chief was a powerful figure, but he needed the support of his people to stay in power. Otherwise he could be replaced.

**Clothing:** The Shawnee made their clothing from animal skins or fur. Shawnee women wore skirts with leggings to keep warm and the men mostly wore leggings. Shirts were not usually worn in the Shawnee culture. The Shawnee sometimes wore beaded headbands with a few feathers. Most Shawnee had long hair, but the warriors sometimes shaved their heads.

**Language:** Shawnee Native Americans all speak English today, but some are trying to keep their Native language alive. It is very song-like and has complicated verbs with many parts. Some easy Shawnee words include "bezon" (pronounced bay-zone), a friendly greeting, and "neahw" (pronounced nay-aw), which means "thank you."

**Food:** Shawnee food included fish and small game like squirrel, deer, raccoon, bear, and beaver. The Shawnee also grew corn (maize), pumpkins, squash, and beans.

**Crafts:** The Shawnee are known for their beadwork, pottery, and woodcarving.

An artist painted settlers looking at land to claim in an area that would become known as Moorfield.

# A Time of War

As more white settlers moved into the region, they took lands belonging to Native Americans, which led to violent clashes. To make matters worse, France and Great Britain had been warring with each other for decades in Europe. That conflict spilled over into North America, and by 1754, Great Britain and France were fighting over territory in the Ohio Valley. The battle in the new land became known as the French and Indian War.

The conflict not only involved France and Great Britain, but also Native Americans who sided with one or the other. Many forts were built to offer settlers protection from the fighting. Some settlements were actually located within the walls of the forts. For example, Fort Blair protected the city now known as Point Pleasant, and Fort Fincastle protected the village of Wheeling.

The French and Indian War came to a close in 1763. Great Britain won and gained all of France's land east of the Mississippi River. After the fighting ended, more settlers came to the region. The British attempted to maintain peace with the Native Americans by forbidding settlers from taking any land west of the Appalachian Mountains. Many settlers ignored this and continued to move westward.

A chief from the Mingo tribe named Logan lived peacefully at first with the new white pioneers. However, in 1773 a group of settlers led by a man named Michael Cresap killed many Shawnee and other Native Americans. In 1774, Cresap's men murdered many peaceful Mingo people, including members of Chief Logan's family. Angered by these attacks, Chief Logan joined forces with a Shawnee chief named Cornstalk to fight the settlers.

This engraving shows a battle from the French and Indian War, which removed France from its lands in most of what is now the United States.

Lord Dunmore, the British governor of the Virginia Colony, sent troops into western Virginia to fight Logan's and Cornstalk's warriors. The conflict became known as Lord Dunmore's War. It ended in 1774 when Dunmore's soldiers defeated the Native Americans at Point Pleasant. After this defeat, many Native American tribes were forced to give up all their land claims south of the Ohio River.

In 1775, settlers across the colonies began fighting for their independence from the British. During the American Revolution, battles were fought throughout the different colonies. Many Native Americans in the Ohio Valley sided with the British. The British encouraged this, hoping to weaken the revolutionary armies.

The American Revolution ended in 1783 with victory for the colonists. A short time afterward, settlers once again began pouring into the area that is now West Virginia, pushing the remaining Native Americans farther west into present-day Indiana. The Native tribes continued to resist, and a huge battle took place in 1794 at Fallen Timbers, in present-day northwestern Ohio. About two thousand Native Americans, including Mingo, Shawnee, Delaware, Ottawa, Miami, and Chippewa warriors, fought against the new US Army led by General Anthony Wayne. The Native Americans were defeated and signed

## Unique Start

Declared a state by President Abraham Lincoln, West Virginia is the only state to be designated by presidential proclamation.

# Making a Thaumatrope

Back in the 1800s, children in West Virginia enjoyed playing with a popular toy called a thaumatrope. They would draw a picture on each side of a disc and put string through holes on either side. When they twirled the disc on the string, the two pictures merged together and appeared as one image, almost like a movie!

You can build your own thaumatrope today!

## What You Need

Cardboard and paper
Two rubber bands
Paper glue
A pair of scissors
A pencil

## What To Do

- Cut two pieces of paper the same size as the cardboard piece.
- Draw a picture on each piece of paper, making it look like one image can fit inside or outside the other (like a fish in a bowl).
- Glue the two pieces of paper to either side of the cardboard, being careful to align the two images with one upside down from the other.
- Make two holes through the paper and the board at opposite sides of the image (on the far right and the far left).
- Insert a rubber band through each hole and grab both ends with each hand.
- Wind up both rubber bands. Pull the rubber bands away from each other quickly and the card will start spinning.
- Your thaumatrope creation is transformed into a single picture by the twisting action.
- Try using different kinds of pictures to make all kinds of new images.

another treaty, giving up all their remaining claims to western Virginia.

## Conflict Between East and West

Life was very different in the eastern and western parts of the new state of Virginia, and residents in one of the sections disagreed with those in the other on many things. Western Virginia was made up of

**You've Got Mail**

The first rural free mail delivery was started in Charles Town on October 6, 1896, and then spread throughout the United States.

frontier farming settlements, while eastern Virginia consisted more of cities and large **plantations**. The eastern plantation owners wielded a great deal of political power in the state. Residents in western Virginia began to feel that they were not well represented in Virginia's government.

Soon an even bigger issue divided east from west—slavery. Big plantations in the east depended upon slave labor to support their agricultural economy. Westerners did not need slaves to run their small farms, and many who lived there thought that slavery was wrong.

One passionate abolitionist, a person who opposed slavery, was a man named John Brown. He and his followers made history when they raided the town of Harpers Ferry, the location of a federal **armory**. Brown hoped to start an armed slave rebellion. He attacked the armory to get weapons for the slaves. United States forces fought back, and

Life in the mountains was very different for residents of western Virginia than for Virginians living closer to the Atlantic Ocean.

John Brown's men were captured and later executed after their raid on the armory at Harpers Ferry

many of John Brown's men were killed—including Brown's son. Brown and the rest of his men were captured and tried in court for treason and murder. Brown was hanged in 1859. Six other raiders were also tried, found guilty, and executed.

Though the raid on Harpers Ferry did not accomplish what Brown had hoped, it did aid the cause of other abolitionists. Brown's actions brought more attention to the issue of slavery, angering people on both sides.

## Torn Apart and Reborn

After the publicity that followed John Brown's failed raid, the slavery question grew in everyone's mind. When Abraham Lincoln was elected president in 1860, he and his Republican Party were strongly against slavery. They wanted to prevent it from spreading into the new western territories. Slaveholders from the Southern states felt the decision to be a free or slave state should be decided by each state, not by the federal government. The idea they supported became known as states' rights. The Southern slaveholders were also concerned Lincoln would not stop at restricting slavery in new western regions. They feared that he would also try to eliminate slavery in the Southern states that already had it.

The issue became so serious that, in 1861, South Carolina voted to secede, or withdraw, from the Union. Other Southern states soon followed, including North Carolina, Georgia, Florida, Arkansas, Tennessee, Alabama, Louisiana, Mississippi, and Texas. The Civil War officially began later in 1861. President Lincoln called for seventy-five thousand volunteers to support the Union and fight in the war.

Virginia was still undecided about secession. Although the majority of western Virginian representatives wanted to stay a part of the Union, the state eventually decided to go along with those in the east who supported slavery. Virginia seceded on April 17, 1861, and then joined the other Southern states to form the Confederacy. A confederacy is a group that agrees to come together to support each other or to do something together. Among the people to join the Confederate cause was Clarksville native Thomas "Stonewall" Jackson. A West Point graduate and one-time professor at Virginia Military Institute, Jackson was a brilliant military leader and organizer. He died of gunshot wounds suffered in a victory at Chancellorsville in May 1863. The shots had been fired by soldiers from the South.

Six months after Virginia seceded, in October 1861, western Virginians decided they had had enough. They chose to break away from Virginia by a vote of 18,408 to 781. On June 20, 1863, President Lincoln signed a bill that admitted West Virginia as the nation's thirty-fifth state.

## Streets of Brick

The first brick street in the world was laid in Charleston, West Virginia, in 1870.

Disagreements caused the state of Virginia to divide during the Civil War, but residents of what became West Virginia fought on both sides.

# ★ 10 KEY CITIES ★ ★

Charleston

We are...
Marsh...
Huntington

## 1. Charleston: population 51,400

Charleston, the largest city in West Virginia, serves as the state capital. Located west of the state's highest elevations where the Elk and Kanawha Rivers meet, Charleston is a center for government, business, education, sports, and the arts.

## 2. Huntington: population 49,138

Sitting on the Ohio River at the point where West Virginia, Ohio, and Kentucky meet, Huntington is part of the largest inland port in the United States. The city is also well known as the home to Marshall University *(bottom left)*.

## 3. Parkersburg: population 31,492

Situated where the Little Kanawha and Ohio Rivers meet, Parkersburg was originally called "Newport" when it was settled at the end of the eighteenth century. Parkersburg boasts several museums as well as the world's oldest producing oil well.

## 4. Morgantown: population 29,660

Located along the Monongahela River, Morgantown sits close to the Pennsylvania border in the north-central part of West Virginia. Morgantown is the home to West Virginia University, the largest institution of higher education in the state.

## 5. Wheeling: population 28,486

Wheeling is located along the Ohio River between Ohio and Pennsylvania in the Northern Panhandle of West Virginia. Wheeling was loyal to the federal government during the Civil War and the state of West Virginia was born here.

# WEST VIRGINIA

## 6. Weirton: population 19,746

A relatively young city incorporated in 1947, Weirton's roots date back to the mid-1700s, when pioneers settled in a valley near the Ohio River offering fresh water and cheap transportation. The city borders two other states, Ohio and Pennsylvania.

## 7. Fairmont: population 18,704

Founded in 1820 as Middletown, the town was nicknamed "Fair Mountain," which was officially shortened to Fairmont, because of its beautiful view above the Monongahela River. Fairmont became a major producer of glass in the early twentieth century.

Fairmont

## 8. Beckley: population 17,614

The largest city in southern West Virginia, Beckley was first settled near old Native American trails. Beckley developed into an important commercial and transportation hub. It now lies at the center of national parklands, rivers, and tourist sites.

## 9. Martinsburg: population 17,227

Located in the heart of the Eastern Panhandle, Martinsburg's location was once the site of the chief town of the Tuscarora Native Americans. Part of West Virginia's fastest growing county, Berkeley, Martinsburg is known as the "Gateway to the Shenandoah Valley."

## 10. Clarksburg: population 16,578

The birthplace of famous Confederate general Stonewall Jackson, Clarksburg was a depot during the Civil War. The Oak Mounds, probably built by the Hopewell culture, are just outside of the city.

Martinsburg

Unlike its neighbors to the east and south, West Virginia experienced relatively few battles on its soil during the Civil War. All in all, more than thirty thousand West Virginia men volunteered for the Union Army. Not everyone in West Virginia supported the Union, though. In fact, about nine thousand West Virginians fought on the side of the Confederacy.

On February 3, 1865, West Virginia abolished slavery. Two months later, the Civil War finally came to an end when a treaty was signed at the Appomattox Court House near Lynchburg, Virginia.

## The Hatfields and the McCoys

A famous family **feud** between two families—the Hatfields and the McCoys—has its roots in the Civil War as well as in West Virginia history. The Hatfields of Logan County, West Virginia, sided with the Confederacy. The McCoys, from across the state line in Kentucky, sided with the Union. A bitter shooting war between the two families began when a pig from one family's farm ran away and was killed, cooked, and eaten by the other. Fighting between the two clans lasted several generations and resulted in a number of killings.

## Industry Grows

Between its admission into the Union and the early 1870s, agriculture was still an important part of West Virginia's economy. Industry soon became important as well, mostly because of improved technology and the state's excellent methods of transportation, including its rivers.

When steam engines could reach places such as Montgomery, they opened West Virginia to trade and tourists.

West Virginia's many rivers served as the state's primary transportation routes. Rivers were the most efficient way for farmers and merchants to get their goods to market. After the Civil War, dams and locks were built on many of the rivers to help control the rivers' depths and flow. The locks were designed to push huge quantities of stored water into shallow parts of the river when boats needed to pass through. This greatly increased river traffic and gave farmers and manufacturers easier and faster ways to haul goods such as produce, timber, clothing, and coal.

Even with improvements in riverboat transportation, there were not enough boats to keep up with West Virginia's booming industries. Bigger and better railroads provided a perfect solution. In 1873, railroad workers completed the Chesapeake and Ohio Railroad in southern West Virginia. It connected the farmland community of Huntington to large cities on the Atlantic coast. Soon other railroad lines were built.

## Coal Becomes King

The coming of the railroads, plus increased industrialization throughout the United States, increased the demand for coal. Coal was plentiful in the many mines of West Virginia. It was used to power train engines and to keep factories running. Thanks to West Virginia's rich coal deposits, coal mining became the state's leading industry. By the late 1880s, the Mountain State's mines yielded more than 1 million tons (907,000 t) of coal.

Many towns were founded near coal mines. The population grew as new **immigrants** from Europe came to the state looking for jobs and the hope for a better life.

Mining companies owned all homes close to the mines in West Virginia. This forced workers to rent from the companies they worked for.

Unfortunately, what they had heard about the coal business and what they actually found were two very different things.

When these new workers arrived to work in the mines, they found that the coal companies were in total control. The companies managed the mines and owned all the equipment. Miners actually had to pay the mining companies to use their tools and live in the housing near the mines. The fees were very high and were often taken out of the miners' pay. As a result, the miners ended up making next to nothing for their hard work in the mines.

Men and boys of all ages had to work in the mines to support their families. Worst of all, the mines were unsafe and the work was extremely dangerous. On December 6, 1907, an explosion at a mine in Monongah killed 361 miners. By then, West Virginia's coal miners were at their breaking point and could take no more. Something had to be done.

## Labor Wars

Across many states, workers from factories, mills, mines, and other industries had been banding together since the 1880s to improve their lives. They wanted to fight the large, controlling companies for better pay and safer working conditions. The groups that came together were called unions. The union created specifically for miners was called the United Mine Workers of America, or UMWA. The UMWA had successfully organized workers in Pennsylvania, Ohio, Indiana, and Illinois. However, unionization in West Virginia was very hard because the mine owners would not allow union people to recruit miners.

A job as a miner meant doing dirty, dangerous, and tiring work.

In 1912, miners at Paint Creek and Cabin Creek walked off the job, setting off a strike. A strike is when workers stop working in order to make one or more demands. Some of the things these miners wanted included the right to organize into a union and get better pay, safer working conditions, and a nine-hour workday.

The strike resulted in violent clashes between the miners and mining companies. Many miners and mine guards were killed. Many others were arrested and sent to prison. When Henry D. Hatfield became governor of West Virginia, he persuaded the mine owners to guarantee that miners would work no more than nine hours per day and to let them organize a union.

World War I helped calm the situation, at least for a short time. When America entered the war in 1917, miners and mine owners cooperated with each other for the good of the country. West Virginia was able to provide its coal to meet the country's fuel needs.

By 1920, two years after World War I ended, the number of West Virginians who had joined the UMWA had grown to fifty thousand workers. Around the same time, the demand for coal increased. Mine owners began to open new mines and improve mining methods.

In 1920, the UMWA attempted to organize miners in Logan and Mingo Counties. The mine owners were determined to stop the unions in those two locations. To prevent unionization, mine owners drove workers from their company-owned homes. The workers were forced to live in tents to keep their jobs. During the winter of 1920–1921, violence once again broke out. Federal troops came in to maintain order.

Despite the presence of troops, the violence continued into the early spring. On May 19, 1921, Governor E. F. Morgan proclaimed a state of martial law in Mingo County, which was known as Bloody Mingo. A few months later, about 3,000 miners from Paint Creek and Cabin Creek went to assist their Mingo County brothers. On August 31, 1921, a force of 1,200 state police and others faced a large group of angry miners outside of Logan. The fighting lasted for four days. Miners from Kentucky, Ohio, and northern West Virginia joined in to help the workers. The fighting grew so intense that President Warren G. Harding sent 2,100 federal troops and US Army airplanes to restore order.

## International Flavor

Many towns in West Virginia are named after cities in other countries, including Athens, Berlin, Cairo, Calcutta, Geneva, Ghent, Glasgow, Killarney, Lima, London, Moscow, Odessa, Ottawa, Palermo, Rangoon, Santiago, Shanghai, Vienna, and Wellington.

The United Mine Workers of America continues to fight for workers, such as these striking members at Pittston, Virginia, in 1989.

Realizing the hopelessness of fighting against the US Army, the miners finally surrendered. Their defeat discouraged further attempts at unionizing the workers. The miners also began to lose confidence in the union itself. As a result, West Virginia's membership in the UMWA dropped from fifty thousand in 1920 to a few hundred by 1932. In 1933, things finally changed for the better for the miners when federal laws recognized the importance of unions and protected them. West Virginia union organizers were once again back in action, only this time they were much more successful.

## Depression, War, and Hope

While West Virginia was involved in violent labor conflicts, much of the rest of the United States was enjoying a period of economic success. In 1929, however, things came to a screeching halt when the stock market crashed. Banks failed across the United States and many people lost their savings and could not pay for their homes. Without money, people could not afford to buy goods, leading many companies that made those goods to collapse. This great slowdown in economic activity eventually brought about the Great Depression.

The Great Depression hit West Virginia especially hard. Wages in the state were already lower than in other places. With factories producing fewer goods nationwide, less coal was needed. Many of West Virginia's miners lost their jobs.

The Great Depression also affected farmers in the state. Many of them ended up losing their land because they could not afford to pay their taxes or the loans they had taken to purchase their farms.

Farmsteads, such as these in Randolph County, were often abandoned during the Great Depression.

The Great Depression touched almost everyone in the United States. To help provide relief for the suffering country, President Franklin D. Roosevelt created a set of programs that would help put people back to work and rebuild the country. These programs came to be known as the "New Deal."

One of President Roosevelt's New Deal employment programs that was very successful in West Virginia was the Civilian Conservation Corps, or CCC. This program gave West Virginia residents the opportunity to work in the state's forests. Some of the jobs they filled included planting millions of trees, developing state and national parks, fighting forest fires, and creating hiking trails through West Virginia's wilderness. More than $7.5 million was spent on the CCC program in West Virginia. It provided housing for the young workers in more than sixty camps that were set up throughout the state.

Another successful New Deal program was the Federal Emergency Relief Administration, or FERA. Under FERA, more than sixty thousand West Virginians were put to work building roads and highways, greatly improving the state's transportation network.

On December 7, 1941, the country of Japan attacked the United States at Pearl Harbor, in Hawaii. This attack brought the United States into World War II. The war actually helped the nation's economy. Fuel, farm products, and other goods were needed for the military troops. Farms, factories, mills, and mines throughout the state were back in business.

This period of productivity did not last long, though. Once World War II ended in 1945, West Virginia seemed to stumble while many other states enjoyed post-war prosperity. Coal production fell drastically as citizens and businesses began to explore other forms of energy, such as gas, oil, and electricity. As a result, once again, thousands of miners lost their jobs.

West Virginia plants and factories have survived tough times.

Disappointed with the constant changes from good times to bad times in the mining business, many people left West Virginia. They went off to search for better opportunities in other states. The state's population dropped in the 1950s and 1960s. Of those who stayed behind, many became unemployed. By the 1980s, West Virginia had the worst unemployment rate in the United States.

Since the 1990s, however, West Virginia has made a comeback. The state government has worked hard to encourage the growth of new businesses and industries. For example, the state government has successfully persuaded computer software companies to move into the state. In addition, the state offered attractive conditions, like low taxes, to encourage the companies to build factories in many West Virginia cities.

Besides the increasing role of the state government in helping the economy, West Virginia's tourism business continues to grow every year. With the unspoiled natural beauty of the state's stunning forests, majestic mountains, and parks—plus the welcoming smiles of its many friendly residents—West Virginia is destined to receive more and more visitors in the years ahead.

The Heritage Farm Museum and Village in Huntington is among the historic sites that attract tourists to the state.

# 10 KEY DATES IN STATE HISTORY

**1. 12,500 BCE**

Paleo-Indians enter the Kanawha River valley in modern-day West Virginia in search of large game, finding mammoths, mastodons, and other ice age animals.

**2. March 9, 1669**

John Lederer, a German geographer hired by the governor of Virginia, sets out on a mission to explore what would become West Virginia.

**3. October 10, 1774**

Native Americans led by Chief Cornstalk are defeated at the Battle of Point Pleasant, forcing the tribes to give up much of their land.

**4. October 16, 1859**

Abolitionist John Brown and twenty-two followers attack the US federal arsenal at Harpers Ferry while trying to incite a slave rebellion and end slavery.

**5. June 20, 1863**

After Virginia joined the Confederacy in 1861, West Virginia separates from Virginia and is admitted into the Union as the thirty-fifth state.

**6. May 10, 1908**

West Virginia resident Ann Maria Reeves Jarvis organizes the first official service for Mother's Day in a Grafton church. It becomes an official holiday in 1914.

**7. August 25–September 2, 1921**

Coal miners clash with 1,200 state police and 2,100 federal troops at Blair Mountain, in the largest labor uprising in US history.

**8. November 14, 1970**

An airplane carrying Marshall University's football team crashes near Ceredo, killing all seventy-five people on board, the deadliest sports-related tragedy in American history.

**9. January 3, 2000**

President Clinton hosts peace talks between Israel and Syria in Shepherdstown. The talks ended with no agreement being reached.

**10. January 9, 2014**

A dangerous chemical spilled into the Elk River, near Charleston, leaves hundreds of thousands of residents without pure drinking water.

Students at West Virginia University help give Morgantown one of the youngest populations in the state.

# The People

According to the 2010 US census, West Virginia's population is just under 1.9 million. Most residents live in the state's rural areas. One of the reasons for the state's large rural population is that the coal mining industry is primarily located in the remote mountains. Since the early 1880s, coal has been one of the major contributors to West Virginia's economy. Families whose members worked the coal mines settled in the mountainous areas close to the mines and away from the cities.

West Virginia's cities tend to be on the small side compared to some larger states. The four largest cities in West Virginia are Charleston, Huntington, Parkersburg, and Morgantown. Charleston, the state's capital and largest industrial center, has a population of approximately fifty-one thousand people. This port city is conveniently located at the junction of the Kanawha and Elk Rivers. Huntington has a population of about forty-nine thousand people. Another small port city, Huntington, sits on the Ohio River near the mouth of the Big Sandy River. Huntington has become the Mountain State's main center of trade and transportation.

Parkersburg is located on the Ohio River at the mouth of the Little Kanawha River. It was founded during West Virginia's late nineteenth-century oil boom. Since then, it has grown into a major manufacturing center where many goods are produced. The city has a population of about thirty-one thousand. The city of Morgantown is home to West Virginia University. It has a population of about thirty thousand. Other major cities include the manufacturing and shipping centers of Wheeling, Fairmont, and Clarksburg.

## Hot Hand

On January 26, 1960, Danny Heater, a student from Burnsville, scored 135 points in a high school basketball game, earning him a place in the *Guinness Book of World Records*

## European Heritage

The first European explorers found a mixture of Native American tribes in present-day West Virginia. As settlers crossed the Allegheny Mountains, conflicts over the Ohio Valley developed between England and France. These conflicts marked the beginning of a forty-year period in which the hunger for land and a preoccupation with frontier defense set the tone for West Virginia affairs.

From the beginning, most Native Americans northwest of the Ohio River favored France, whose interests in the fur trade posed little threat to Native American land or ways of life. On the other hand, English settlements and farms took over tribal lands and posed a danger that had to be resisted. Great Britain's victory over France hurt the position of tribes that supported the losing side. As more European settlers came to the area, Native Americans were forced to move away from their traditional homes.

## Little Diversity

Partly because of that history, West Virginia's present racial mix is not very diverse, even today. Most West Virginians reported a single-race

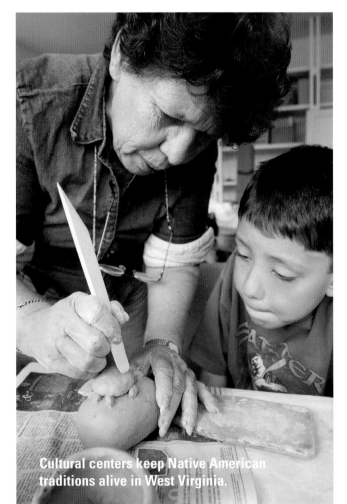
Cultural centers keep Native American traditions alive in West Virginia.

background in the 2010 census, with just 1.5 percent of the state's residents reporting more than one race.

West Virginia's citizens are mostly white, about 94 percent of the total population. Many of these residents are descendants of the settlers who came to the area hundreds of years ago. By the mid-eighteenth century, settlers of European descent had begun to settle in the territory that eventually became West Virginia, most numerously in the Eastern Panhandle and Potomac Highlands regions. These included new immigrants, as well as others who were related to colonial settlers who came from Virginia, Pennsylvania, New York, New Jersey, Delaware, and Maryland.

These settlers were primarily of German and Scots-Irish origins, although there were significant numbers of English and other nationalities, as well. Later, at the turn of the twentieth century, immigrants from Ireland, Italy, Poland, and Hungary also arrived in the state, seeking work in the growing coal, lumber, and manufacturing industries. Some of the descendants of these later arrivals can still be found today in West Virginia's coal-mining regions and industrial centers. Their rich culture and traditions are very much alive, too. Examples include Lewis County's Irish Spring Festival and Clarksburg's Italian Heritage Festival.

According to the 2010 census, people of Hispanic or Latino heritage make up about 1.3 percent of the state's population, and only 0.7 percent reported their race as Asian. Native Americans, who were once the only people living in the region, make up an even smaller portion of the population at only 0.2 percent.

Smaller communities such as Lewisburg provide a great lifestyle to West Virginia residents.

# ★ 10 ★ KEY PEOPLE ★ ★

### 1. Pearl S. Buck

Pearl S. Buck was born in Hillsboro, West Virginia, in 1892, but spent many years in China. Her second novel, *The Good Earth*, earned her a Pulitzer Prize in 1932. She was also the fourth woman to win a Nobel Prize for Literature.

### 2. Vicky Bullett

Born in 1967 in Martinsburg, Vicki Bullett grew up playing basketball with her six brothers. She starred in high school, college, the Olympics, and professionally, and was inducted into the Women's Basketball Hall of Fame in 2011.

Vicky Bullett

### 3. Chris Cline

Chris Cline grew up in Beckley, West Virginia. He dropped out of Marshall University to work in the family coal business and is now known as the "New King Coal." This billionaire has made large donations to promote higher education in West Virginia.

### 4. Homer Hickam

Born in 1943 in Coalwood, Homer Hickam loved to build rockets. He and some friends won gold and silver medals at the 1960 National Science Fair with their rocket designs. Hickam went on to work for NASA.

Homer Hickam

### 5. Brad Paisley

Country music star Brad Paisley was born in Glen Dale in 1972. His grandfather taught him how to play the guitar, inspiring a deep love of music. Paisley has sold millions of recordings around the world.

Brad Paisley

# WEST VIRGINIA

## 6. Mary Lou Retton

When she was sixteen, Fairmont's Mary Lou Retton became famous during the 1984 Summer Olympics, winning the gold medal for all-around gymnastic performance. She was the first American gymnast to win Olympic gold in thirty-six years.

## 7. Cynthia Rylant

Born in Hopewell, Cynthia Rylant is a children's writer who won a Newbery Medal for her book *Missing May*. Her first work, *When I Was Young in the Mountains*, describes her childhood in the Appalachian region of West Virginia.

## 8. Booker T. Washington

Born into slavery in 1856, Booker T. Washington grew up in Malden, West Virginia. He earned a college degree at Hampton Institute. His accomplishments include founding the Tuskegee Institute, a college dedicated to serving black youth, and the National Negro Business League.

## 9. Jerry West

Jerry West led East Bank High School to a state basketball title, and West Virginia University to the NCAA final. He won championships with the Los Angeles Lakers as a player and general manager before his election to the Basketball Hall of Fame.

## 10. Chuck Yeager

Chuck Yeager, born in Myra in 1923, was a World War II fighter pilot who became a test pilot after the war. In 1947, he became the first pilot to fly faster than the speed of sound.

Mary Lou Retton

Booker T. Washington

Jerry West

# Who West Virginians Are

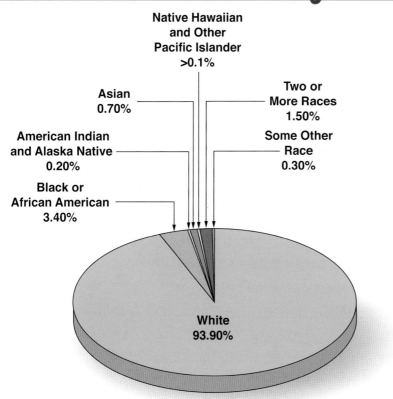

Native Hawaiian and Other Pacific Islander
>0.1%

Asian
0.70%

American Indian and Alaska Native
0.20%

Black or African American
3.40%

Two or More Races
1.50%

Some Other Race
0.30%

White
93.90%

**Total Population**
**1,852,994**

Hispanic or Latino (of any race):
• 22,268 (1.2%))

**Note:** The pie chart shows the racial breakdown of the state's population based on the categories used by the US Bureau of the Census. The Census Bureau reports information for Hispanics or Latinos separately, since they may be of any race. Percentages in the pie chart may not add to 100 because of rounding.

Source: US Bureau of the Census, 2010 Census

## African Americans

Large farms and plantations were not as plentiful in what would become West Virginia as they were in other states, particularly Virginia and others farther south. Therefore, before the Civil War, slavery was not common in most parts of western Virginia. There were some exceptions in the major river valleys, including the Greenbrier, Kanawha, and Ohio valleys, and in the Eastern Panhandle. In other cases, some industries, including the salt works of Kanawha County, did use slaves for labor. Generally speaking, however, the African-American population in West Virginia was lower than in other Southern states when the Civil War ended.

After the Civil War, the coal industry began to grow quickly. This attracted many African Americans to the new state, along with a variety of European immigrants. Many African Americans worked in the coal mines, especially in the southern part of the state, including those in McDowell, Fayette, and Mercer Counties.

Today, African Americans make up only about 3.4 percent of West Virginia's population. Some have descended directly from ancestors who worked in the coal mines. A small percentage of West Virginia's African Americans are also descendants of the slaves who were brought to the state before the Civil War.

The mining boom brought many African-American families to West Virginia. Many of these families stayed in the state.

All West Virginians—no matter what their background may be—play important roles in the state. Besides sharing their heritage and culture through events around the state, they also play an important role in the state's economy. This rich mixture of history, culture, and industry helps to make the Mountain State strong.

## Getting Older

The state's population has grown older during the past century. According to the 2010 census, West Virginia's **median age** (41.3) is much higher than the nation's (37.2). The median age is the one at which half of the people are younger and half are older. West Virginia has not always had a higher median age than the country. In fact, it usually finished lower. In the year 1950, for example, West Virginia's median age was about four years below the national average (26.3 compared to 30.2). These figures also point out how the population is aging over the years.

West Virginia's aging population has been caused in part by the fact that many young residents left the state when the economy declined in the 1980s. The median age is not the same across the state. It varies from one section to the next. The northwestern and southeastern areas tend to be older, while residents of the Eastern Panhandle and the southwestern part of the state are on average usually younger. Pendleton County has the highest median age, at 47.3 years. Monongalia County has the lowest median age in the state, at 29.1 years. This reflects the college student population at West Virginia University. Monongalia County was the only county in West Virginia with a median age below the US average.

# The Christian Influence

While West Virginia has a diversity of religious beliefs and practices, residents who identify themselves as religious are overwhelmingly Christian and very largely Protestant. The largest **denomination** in the state is United Methodist. American Baptist and Roman Catholics are also well represented. Other Christian denominations are present as well. There are also small Jewish and Muslim populations, and others adhering to non-Western religions.

West Virginia's religious makeup is largely a product of the state's history. As early settlers made their way into the western wilderness, they carried their religious beliefs and practices with them. Since many of these settlers claimed a Scots-Irish heritage, Presbyterianism was the dominant form of Christianity in the early years. However, Baptists and Methodists later gained thousands of converts and have been the largest Christian denominations in West Virginia ever since.

After the Civil War, a growing number of newcomers arrived, attracted by the growth of jobs in new industries. Many immigrants from southern and eastern Europe, often Catholics, settled in the mining and manufacturing regions, some of them establishing Eastern Orthodox congregations.

A significant number of Jews immigrated to West Virginia during the same period, and synagogues were established throughout the state. Muslims came as well, initially living quietly among mostly Christian neighbors. Their numbers increased in the twentieth century, and mosques were established in South Charleston and elsewhere.

While the majority of West Virginia remains Christian and Protestant, West Virginia's religious landscape continues to change. Groups once uncommon in the state continue to make inroads as West Virginia, and the country as a whole, becomes more diverse.

# Education

Education is very important to West Virginians. Taxpayers do their best to provide a good education for all students, no matter where they live. Local primary and high schools serve as vital centers for community activities, hosting youth sports such as basketball and football, as well as public meetings and cultural events such as concerts and plays.

The West Virginia Board of Education was established in the West Virginia Constitution. The Board is responsible for the general supervision of the state's elementary and secondary schools. The board includes twelve members, nine of whom are citizens appointed by the governor. The board meets every month to discuss educational policies for the schools under its jurisdiction and to establish rules that affect state education.

Most colleges in West Virginia are small to midsize in student population and include a mix of research universities, liberal arts colleges, and several small private Christian colleges. West Virginia University in Morgantown is the state's largest traditional university, though only about 50 percent of students are West Virginia residents. The others come from other states, usually those located nearby. A few top colleges in West Virginia can be found in the state capital of Charleston, which is located in the central part of the state.

Residents of West Virginia can also attend select colleges and universities in nearby states, including Virginia, Kentucky, Maryland and Tennessee. To make it easier for students to consider attending colleges that suit their interests, these states have formed a connection that allows residents in each state to attend a college in a neighboring state while still paying the lower tuition granted to in-state residents. This arrangement allows students in West Virginia to widen their horizons when choosing a college while still taking advantage of lower in-state tuitions.

## Sports

No major league professional teams are based in West Virginia, but there are minor league baseball teams in cities like Charleston, Bluefield, and Princeton, and a minor league hockey team in Wheeling. Many West Virginians also root for professional teams from nearby cities in neighboring states, including Pittsburgh (Pennsylvania), Baltimore (Maryland) and Washington, DC.

College and high school sports are also very popular in West Virginia. The West Virginia Mountaineers compete in all sports in the Big 12 Conference, while the Marshall University Thundering Herd play in the East Division of Conference USA. Both conferences are members of the National Collegiate Athletic Association.

## Outdoor Activities

West Virginia is the place to be if you love the outdoors. The state has many streams for fishing, rivers for rafting, and wilderness areas for hiking, horseback riding, rock climbing, and hunting. Residents and tourists like to swim, boat, and visit the state's national parks. In the winter, there is powdery snow for skiing, snowboarding, and snowmobiling. Ski slopes and backcountry trails are full of West Virginians and others enjoying a winter's day.

Around the state, there are festivals of all kinds, honoring ethnic heritage, state history, and religious holidays.

# ★ 10 KEY EVENTS ★

## 1. Berkeley Springs International Water Tasting

Each February, this festival welcomes more than one hundred waters from across the country and around the globe. Held in the historic spa town of Berkeley Springs, it is the largest water tasting competition in the world.

## 2. Blue and Gray Reunion

One of the first battles of the Civil War was fought over Barbour County's Philippi Bridge, which is West Virginia's longest and oldest covered bridge. The bridge still stands, and every June volunteers reenact the historic fight that took place.

## 3. Fall Children's Festival

Held each October at the West Virginia Botanic Garden in Morgantown, this festival is a true family event. It features craft demonstrations and seasonal treats. Kids can build their own fairy houses, paint pumpkins, and enjoy delicious seasonal refreshments.

## 4. Gardner Winter Music Festival

Visitors can get a strong sense of West Virginia's musical heritage at the Gardner Winter Music Festival, held in late February. The festival showcases traditional Appalachian music performed by musicians from West Virginia and other nearby states.

## 5. Irish Spring Festival

Ireland, a town in Lewis County, was founded in the early 1800s by Irishman Andrew Wilson. He lived to be 114 years old. To honor his long life and the town's Irish heritage, the town holds a weeklong celebration.

Berkeley Springs International Water Tasting

Blue and Gray Reunion

## 6. Italian Heritage Festival

Every Labor Day weekend, Clarksburg pays tribute to West Virginia's Italian Americans with this fun-filled event, which attracts more than one hundred thousand visitors each year. The event features authentic Italian food, top-name entertainers, and games for all ages.

## 7. Leaf Peepers Festival

This event in Tucker County is held in late September, when West Virginia's forests are ablaze with bright autumn colors of orange, red, and yellow. Besides leaf peeping, visitors can enjoy the area's food, crafts, and live music.

## 8. Mountain State Forest Festival

A tradition since 1930, this eight-day fall event in Elkins presents a variety of shows, exhibitions, and competitions, many of them related to the forest theme. It is the largest and oldest festival in the state.

## 9. State Fair of West Virginia

Held in Lewisburg each August, the State Fair of West Virginia has been popular for more than eighty-six years, attracting more than two hundred thousand annual visitors. Among its attractions are a carnival and competitive farmers' exhibitions.

## 10. West Virginia Black Walnut Festival

When local resident Henry Young sold 2 million pounds (907,000 kilograms) of black walnuts in 1954, the residents of Spencer thought it was a good reason to celebrate. The festival has grown to become a four-day mid-October event.

Italian Heritage Festival

West Virginia Black Walnut Festival

The interior of Independence Hall
in Wheeling has been restored.
West Virginia's first constitution
was drawn up here.

# How the Government Works

The government of West Virginia was created when the Civil War led to a split in the state of Virginia between people who supported the Union and those who wanted to join the Confederacy. The western counties of Virginia organized the new state with the adoption of its first constitution, and in 1863, West Virginia became the thirty-fifth state of the United States.

The new state experienced difficulty until its present constitution was adopted in 1872, resolving disagreements between the formerly Confederate east and south and the Unionist north. The 1872 constitution, which has since been revised with newer amendments, still serves as the basic law of the state.

Like all states, West Virginia has many levels of government. On the most local level, citizens of towns and cities elect their own officials to manage the affairs in their area. Many cities and towns in the Mountain State are led by a mayor or manager, and by council members. These local governments often handle issues such as zoning or land use.

At the next level, West Virginia's towns and cities are grouped to form counties. West Virginia is divided into fifty-five counties. Each county is managed by a county commission. Each commission is made up of three commissioners who are elected to serve six-year terms. The commissioners oversee county responsibilities such as maintaining parks and roads controlled by the county, as well as providing local police protection and library services. Other county officials include the sheriff (the chief law enforcement officer), the prosecuting attorney, the tax assessor, the circuit clerk, the county clerk, and the land surveyor. All serve four-year terms.

## From Local to State

West Virginia is headed by a governor who is elected to a four-year term. The Mountain State also has thirty-four state senators and one hundred delegates. Each senator or delegate represents a specific region, or district, in the state.

The state government passes laws and adopts policies on issues that affect the whole state. State government responsibilities include setting statewide education policies, maintaining law and order, providing emergency services, and overseeing basic services such as transportation, communication, and water. The city of Wheeling served as the state's first capital. Charleston was declared the permanent capital in 1877.

The state of West Virginia is represented at the federal level in Washington, DC. Eligible voters elect two senators to serve six-year terms in the US Senate. Based on its population, West Virginia also elects three members of the House of Representatives to serve two-year terms.

## Branches of Government

The state government has three branches—executive, legislative, and judicial.

### Executive

West Virginia's executive branch is charged with making sure that the state's laws are carried out. A governor, who may serve no more than two terms in a row, heads up the executive branch. The governor has the power to veto, or to reject, laws or parts of laws that the state legislature passes. As chief executive of the state, he or she also has the power to prepare a budget, choose department heads, call out the National Guard during emergencies, and also direct other important functions.

> ## In Their Own Words
>
> "My solution would be to bridge the skills gap, such as coal to gas training ... You have to give people a sense of hope that they have the tools to be able to diversify and stay in the community where they wish to live."
> —Senator Shelley Moore Capito

Confederate general Stonewall Jackson, born in Clarksburg, is honored with a statue near the capitol in Charleston.

The executive branch also includes the secretary of state; the auditor, who supervises the state's finances and budget; and the state attorney general. Like the governor, each is elected to a four-year term. Unlike many states, West Virginia does not have a lieutenant governor. The president of the state senate stands next in line to replace the governor if needed.

## Legislative

West Virginia's legislative branch is in charge of making and amending, or changing, the state's laws. The legislature is divided into two houses: the Senate and the House of Delegates. When both houses agree on a bill, it is sent to the governor for his or her signature. Once the governor signs the bill, it becomes law.

## Judicial

The judicial branch of West Virginia's state government is responsible for interpreting the laws that the state's legislature passes. West Virginia's highest court is the State Supreme Court of Appeals, which rules on whether laws are in agreement with West Virginia's constitution. The judicial branch also includes circuit, magistrate, and municipal courts.

Legislators debate and pass laws in this chamber in the capitol.

# From Bill to Law

West Virginia's elected representatives often write and propose bills in response to the concerns of ordinary citizens. The process follows five principal stages: committee action, floor action, committee in the second chamber action, conference committee action, and action by the governor.

Before a delegate introduces a bill, the clerk of the senate or house identifies the bill with a number. That number is used to refer to the bill throughout the period of consideration. Once the bill is numbered, the president of the senate or the speaker of the house gives the bill to a standing committee. A standing committee is a small group of senators or delegates who are assigned to study bills about specific subjects. For example, one senate standing committee might be made up of senators who are experts in crime control. This process enables more bills to be studied because they go directly to those who are experts in their field.

After the standing committee examines the bill, the committee files a written report. The report will state whether the committee recommends passing the bill—perhaps with

## Silly Law

In West Virginia, it is against the law to snooze on a train.

amendments, or changes—or rejecting it. Some bills "die in committee." That means the committee members may not have had the time needed to study the bill, or they may have decided the bill should not be recommended to the other members of the senate or house for action.

If the committee recommends passing the bill, it is then reported to the members of the house or the senate, where it is read three times. During the first reading, the members of the house or senate are simply told that a bill is about to be considered. On the second reading, members vote on the amendments suggested by the committee, as well as the amendments individual members of the house or senate may have proposed. Voting on the passage of the bill takes place during the third reading. If a bill passes in one house, it is sent to the other and the process is repeated.

If the second house makes changes to a bill, it is sent back to the first house to see if its members agree with the changes. If they do not agree and the second house refuses to remove the changes, a conference committee is called. The conference committee is made up of an equal number of members from each house. Their job is to try to work things out.

If the conference committee reaches a compromise, both houses must adopt its ruling and vote on the bill again. After a bill passes both houses, it is sent to the governor, who either signs the bill into law or vetoes (rejects) it. If the governor vetoes the bill, the legislature may vote to override the veto. If the legislature then reaches a majority vote in favor of passing the bill, it can override the governor's veto. When that happens, the bill becomes law without the governor's approval.

Many ideas for laws come from ordinary citizens. It is the job of the state legislators to listen to the residents' concerns and ideas. If you have an issue that you think is important to your state, do not be afraid to talk about it. You can ask your parents, teachers, or media specialists to help you research the issue and how to bring it to the attention of your state legislators.

## Robert Byrd: US Senator, 1959-2010

Senator Robert Byrd was the longest-serving US senator and, including his time in the House of Representatives, was also the longest-serving member in the history of the United States Congress. After opposing the Civil Rights Act in 1964, he later battled against racial intolerance.

## Shelley Moore Capito: US Congresswoman, 2001-2015, US Senator, 2015-

A lifelong West Virginian, Shelly Moore Capito was elected to the United States Senate in 2014, becoming the first female US senator in West Virginia's history. She previously served in the US House of Representatives and West Virginia State Legislature. She voted to expand educational benefits for veterans of the military.

## Earl Ray Tomblin: Governor, 2011-

Earl Ray Tomblin became governor of West Virginia in November 2011 after then-Governor Joseph Manchin left office to become a US senator. Tomblin was reelected in November 2012. Formerly a businessman and teacher, Governor Tomblin also served in the West Virginia State Legislature.

# WEST VIRGINIA
## YOU CAN MAKE A DIFFERENCE

## Contacting Lawmakers

To find out more about the West Virginia Legislature, go to their educational website at:

**www.legis.state.wv.us/Educational/citizens/guide.cfm**.

This citizen's guide provides all kinds of information about the state legislature and its processes. You can also search for house and senate lawmakers by name or district by utilizing interactive district maps on the site.

## Helping Missing Children

After a West Virginia teenager vanished from her home and was later found murdered, her parents worked with the state legislature to pass "Skylar's Law." The new law made it easier for other families to find their missing children.

Sixteen-year-old Skylar Neese left her home one night in July 2012. When she did not return home by the next morning, her worried parents called the police. They wanted the authorities to use the AMBER Alert program to help find Skylar. This program alerts the public to look for children who have been kidnapped. The police thought Skylar may have run away from home, so they did not use an AMBER Alert.

Skylar Neese's body was found months later. She was murdered by two schoolmates. Despite their grief, her parents worked with their state representatives to change the rules and use AMBER Alerts for all missing children.

Representatives in the state legislature agreed and passed a new bill. In May 2013, the governor signed a law that requires authorities to turn information over to AMBER Alert officials even when police suspect a child may be a runaway. The law was named "Skylar's Law" in honor of Skylar Neese.

The National Instant Criminal Background Check System in the Federal Bureau of Investigation building in Clarksburg is one of the high-tech government facilities that put West Virginians to work.

# Making a Living

For a state blessed with natural beauty and so many resources, West Virginia has had its share of economic ups and downs. Despite their state's problems, however, West Virginians always seem to overcome their obstacles and move their state forward.

## Agriculture

West Virginia has very little flat land, so it is very difficult to grow crops there. However, up until the late 1800s, most West Virginians depended upon farming for their livelihood. Families continued to rely upon their fields and the forests for products commonly used in their food, shelter, and clothing. Early industries, including grain milling and textile manufacturing, were often farm related.

Today, agriculture represents only a small percentage of the state's economy. Despite this, farms cover more than 3 million acres (1.2 million hectares) of West Virginia land. That is about one-fifth of the state's total land area. Many of these farms are livestock farms or ranches. They raise sheep, turkeys, chickens, and cattle for meat and dairy products.

Among West Virginia's major cash crops are tobacco, corn, and hay. The Eastern Panhandle region is also well known for its peach and apple orchards. In fact, the golden

Agriculture is not a big part of West Virginia's economy, but many small farms thrive in the state.

delicious apple was first introduced in the United States by farmers from West Virginia's Eastern Panhandle.

## From Farms to Mines

The War of 1812 stimulated industrial development, especially for salt and iron. By 1815, fifty-two salt furnaces were operating along the Kanawha River for a distance of 10 miles (16.1 km) east of Charleston. The area surrounding Wheeling and the Monongahela valley became important centers of iron manufacturing. The production of salt and iron stimulated growth in other industries, including timbering, flatboat construction, barrel making, and coal mining.

Although coal was known to exist throughout much of West Virginia, no extensive mining took place until the early 1800s. By 1817, coal began to replace charcoal and wood as a fuel for homes, ships, and industries. The formation of large coal mining operations soon followed.

On the eve of the Civil War, Burning Springs in Wirt County emerged as one of the first important oil fields in the United States. Natural gas, often found in the same locations as oil, had little importance before the war. During the 1840s, however, William Tompkins, a Kanawha valley salt maker, experimented with using natural gas to operate his salt wells.

## Rivers and Railroads

As West Virginia's industry and population grew, better methods of transportation had to be developed to move people and goods. The National Road, the first major highway in the region, was completed by the federal government from Cumberland, Maryland, to

Much of West Virginia's coal is still transported on river barges.

Wheeling in 1818. The highway helped to transform Wheeling into a major industrial and commercial center in the upper Ohio Valley. As more roads were completed, numerous new towns were settled and the economy continued to grow.

When steamboats began to replace older boats on West Virginia's rivers, steamboat construction quickly became an important industry along the upper Ohio. Steamboats also required better river conditions. In the 1850s, the Coal River Navigation Company, with support from coal companies and the state, built nine locks and dams, the first in what was then western Virginia.

By the 1830s, railroads began to attract more attention across the country. The first major rail line in western Virginia, the Baltimore & Ohio, was completed from Harpers Ferry to Wheeling in 1853. Railroad construction continued to expand, especially after the Civil War.

World War I helped to stimulate many industries, especially chemical manufacturing. New products included rubber, plastics, rayon, nylon, and automotive antifreezes. West Virginia's Kanawha valley became one of the chemical centers of the world. By 1970, every Ohio River county except Jackson boasted at least one chemical plant. Production of textiles, clay products, glass, and electric power also grew rapidly.

Since that time, West Virginia's once-flourishing coal mining and steel manufacturing industries have suffered downturns as the nation's economy changed and foreign competition increased. Coal production dropped dramatically after World War II, when industries switched to other sources of energy such as gas and oil. More recently, concerns about the environment have led many to other sources of energy and further away from coal.

Automotive

Chemicals

## 1. Aerospace

The aerospace industry is one of the fastest-growing divisions of the state economy. Raw materials account for more than half of total aerospace production costs, and West Virginia provides an abundant supply of metal products used in the industry.

## 2. Automotive

West Virginia is home to many automotive manufacturers, including Toyota, NGK Spark Plugs, and Diamond Electric. The fact that the Center for Alternative Fuels Engines and Emissions is located at West Virginia University is a contributing factor.

## 3. Biotech

Home to leading companies like Dow and DuPont, West Virginia contains one of the nation's largest concentrations of **biotech** industries. These biotech products include the area of agricultural feedstock, as well as the chemical and pharmaceutical industries.

## 4. Chemicals

West Virginia is home to about 140 different chemical-related companies that provide more than 12,800 jobs to the state. This makes West Virginia the location of one of the largest groups of chemical manufacturing companies in the world.

## 5. Coal

Coal has long been identified with West Virginia. In the late 1890s, most people came to the state to work in the coal mines. Though production is declining, West Virginia still produced more than 113 million tons (103 million t) of coal in 2013.

# WEST VIRGINIA

### 6. Glassware

West Virginia was attractive to glass manufacturers because it offered plentiful sources of fuel and great quantities of silica sand, stone, and other materials used for producing glass. West Virginia glassmakers are known for their figurines, sculptures, cups, and stained-glass windows.

### 7. Golden Delicious Apples

West Virginia farmers introduced the golden delicious apple in the United States. The inside of this crisp apple is sweet and juicy. The golden delicious apple is perfect for cooking, especially in making applesauce and apple juice.

### 8. Limestone

West Virginia was once covered by seas and lakes. Many minerals, such as calcite, collected at the bottom of these bodies of water. Limestone comes from rocks that are made from calcite. It is used to build roads and other concrete structures.

### 9. Natural Gas

Natural gas is one of the state's most important resources. It is mined and used for energy that heats homes and provides power. Natural gas is found in the hills of the central and west-central regions of the state.

### 10. Salt

Salt mining was West Virginia's first important industry. The state's salt deposits are found deep underground, with the richest mines located in Marshall County. West Virginia salt is shipped all over the world.

Glassware

Limestone

# Recipe for Apple Butter

West Virginia is famous for its apples and its delicious apple recipes, including apple butter. Berkeley Springs holds its famous Apple Butter Festival every year on Columbus Day weekend.

Despite its name, apple butter does not have any butter in it. It's actually a delicious paste made from cooked apples and spices. Spread it on just about anything from bread to crackers.

You can make your own delicious apple butter at home.

## What You Need

12 medium cooking apples, peeled and cut into fourths

1½ cups (355 milliliters) packed brown sugar

½ cup (118 mL) apple juice

1 tablespoon (15 mL) ground cinnamon

1 tablespoon (15 mL) lemon juice

1 teaspoon (5 mL) ground allspice

1 teaspoon (5 mL) ground nutmeg

½ teaspoon (2.5 mL) ground cloves

## What To Do

- Mix all ingredients in a 5- to 6-quart (4.75- to 5.7-liter) slow cooker.
- Cover and cook on low heat setting eight to ten hours or until apples are very tender.
- Mash apples with potato masher or large fork.
- Cook uncovered on low heat setting one to two hours, stirring occasionally, until mixture is very thick. Cool about two hours.
- Spoon apple butter into container. Cover and store in refrigerator up to three weeks.

In the 1990s, however, the state's economy showed signs of improvement. Important growth areas included certain areas of manufacturing, such as the automobile and wood-based industries; service industries; tourism; and recreation. By 1996, the state's improved economy seemed to be contributing to a reversal of nearly four decades of population losses. Today, West Virginia's mining, manufacturing, and service industries seem to be in better shape.

Industry, including mining and manufacturing, still makes up a major part of the state's economic profits. The Mountain State's most valuable mineral resource is still coal. West Virginia is the nation's second-leading coal-producing state, just behind Wyoming.

As technology has improved, mining companies have found more efficient ways to mine coal. Unfortunately, in some ways, this improved machinery has made life hard for miners in the state. While the new equipment helps them mine more coal at a faster rate, it also results in the need for fewer miners. Consequently, some of West Virginia's richest coal-mining regions, particularly those in the southern portion of the state, have been hit with high rates of unemployment.

The miners are not the only ones who lose their jobs. People who live and work around the mining communities also suffer when there are fewer people living—and spending money—near the mines.

West Virginia has other valuable natural resources. Natural gas, which is used for energy, is becoming more and more important in the state. Limestone can be found in West Virginia's rocks. The limestone is collected and used for construction in the state and around the country. Sand and gravel found in the state—much of it taken from the bottom

Coal still provides jobs and money to people and companies in West Virginia.

of the Ohio River—are also used in construction. The state's many forests provide wood for the lumber industry.

Chemical manufacturing also remains an important West Virginia industry. Factories in the state manufacture many important products, including paints, plastics, detergents, and dyes.

To make sure that the state's economy stays healthy, state governmental officials have worked to attract newer businesses to the state. Thanks to their efforts, numerous computer software companies have moved into an area between Morgantown and Clarksburg. This had led some Mountain State residents to call that region Software Valley.

Many federal government operations have moved from Washington, DC, to West Virginia. For example, the Fingerprint Center of the Federal Bureau of Investigation, or FBI, is now a major employer in Clarksburg. In addition, the Computing Center of the Internal Revenue Service, or IRS—the government agency that collects income taxes—has opened in Martinsburg.

Natural gas is found in several regions of the state.

## Personal Services and Tourism

More than half of the money that makes up West Virginia's economy comes from the state's service industries. The service industry includes any jobs that provide a service for people instead of making a product that can be sold. Examples of service industry workers include teachers, sales clerks, librarians, insurance agents, doctors, real estate agents, bankers, and tour guides. More than half of the jobs in West Virginia are service jobs.

The most important service industry in the Mountain State is tourism. In 2013, tourists spent more than $4 billion and directly supported about 44,400 jobs. West Virginia has plenty to offer, especially for those who love outdoor activities. During the winter months, the state's breathtaking mountains attract many skiers. White-water rafting is another popular sport, and West Virginia's many fast-flowing rivers give visitors a lot of opportunities. There are also plenty of activities for those who enjoy hiking, camping, boating, fishing, and rock climbing. People who come to do these fun outdoor activities spend money in the state for food, lodging, souvenirs, and sporting equipment.

Rock climbers are drawn to West Virginia's mountains and cliffs.

Visitors are also drawn to the state's many indoor activities. A popular destination is the John Brown Wax Museum in Harpers Ferry. Visitors learn about John Brown's attempt to start a slave rebellion and end slavery. Another popular tourist site is the Oil and Gas Museum in Parkersburg. The exhibits there feature engines, equipment, and tools used in the early days of the state's oil and gas industry.

West Virginia has other historical sites that attract many people every year. From colonial sites to pioneer villages to Native American culture centers, visitors can come to the state and learn about West Virginia's history.

West Virginia's many restaurants, hotels, and entertainment sites are also an important part of the service industry. Residents and visitors spend money to dine, shop, and enjoy other fun activities in the state's busy cities and towns.

Thanks to the efforts of all of West Virginia's hard-working people, the state has faced good times and hard times and come out stronger. It is West Virginians' spirit of dedication, passion, ingenuity, and old-fashioned friendliness that will create a very bright future for the Mountain State in the years ahead.

# WEST VIRGINIA
## STATE MAP

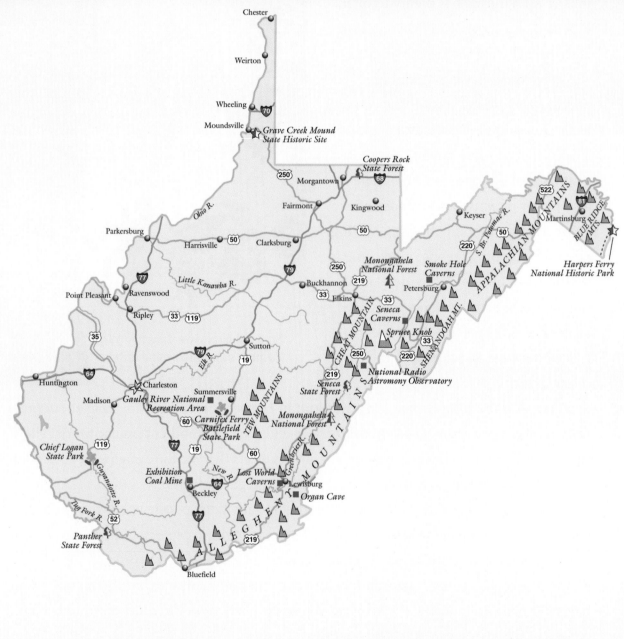

Chester

Weirton

Wheeling
70

Moundsville
Grave Creek Mound
State Historic Site

Coopers Rock
State Forest

250
Morgantown
68

Fairmont
Kingwood

Keyser

522

81
Martinsburg

Ohio R.
Parkersburg

Harrisville
50
Clarksburg

50

BLUE RIDGE MTS.

Harpers Ferry
National Historic Park

S. Br. Potomac R.
50

220

APPALACHIAN MOUNTAINS

79

250

Monongahela
National Forest

Smoke Hole
Caverns

Buckhannon

219

Petersburg

33
Elkins

Little Kanawha R.

Point Pleasant
Ravenswood

33
Seneca
Caverns

33
220

SHENANDOAH MT.

Ripley
33
119

CHEAT MOUNTAIN
Spruce Knob

35

Sutton
250
219

National Radio
Astronomy Observatory

79

19

Elk R.

NEW MOUNTAINS

Seneca
State Forest

Huntington
64
Charleston

Madison

Summersville
Gauley River National
Recreation Area

Carnifex Ferry
Battlefield
State Park

60

Monongahela
National Forest

ALLEGHENY MOUNTAINS

Chief Logan
State Park

119

77

19

60

Greenbrier R.

Exhibition
Coal Mine

New R.

Lost World
Caverns

64

Lewisburg

Organ Cave

Beckley

Gwyandotte R.

Tug Fork R.
52

Panther
State Forest

ALLEGHENY MOUNTAINS

77

219

Bluefield

### Legend

| | | |
|---|---|---|
| Interstate | State Capital | National Forest |
| Major Highway | Highest Point in State | State Forest |
| Appalachian Trail | Mountains | State Park |
| City or Town | Historic Site | Other Points of Interest |

0    mi    50
km
100

# WEST VIRGINIA
## MAP SKILLS

1. What is the highest point in West Virginia?

2. What city lies farthest west in West Virginia?

3. What interstate highway crosses the short distance between Wheeling and West Virginia's eastern border?

4. What famous site is located closest to Beckley?

5. What two rivers meet at Parkersburg?

6. What National Historic Park can be found just east of the Blue Ridge Mountains?

7. What three interstate highways meet at West Virginia's capital city?

8. Bluefield sits at the southern end of what mountain range in southern West Virginia?

9. What is the closest city to Smoke Hole Caverns?

10. What West Virginia state park bears the name of a famous Native American tribal chief?

Charleston

Smoke Hole Caverns

10. Chief Logan State Park
9. Petersburg
8. Allegheny Mountains
7. Interstates 64, 77, and 79
6. Harpers Ferry National Historic Park
5. The Ohio River and the Little Kanawha River
4. Exhibition Coal Mine
3. Interstate 70
2. Huntington
1. Spruce Knob

# State Flag, Seal, and Song

West Virginia adopted its present state flag on March 7, 1929. The background, or field, of the flag is pure white bordered by a strip of blue. In the center is the coat of arms of the state of West Virginia. A horseshoe-like arrangement of rhododendrons, the state flower, surrounds most of the seal.

The Great Seal of West Virginia was adopted by the legislature on September 26, 1863. The seal bears the legend "State of West Virginia," together with the motto "Montani Semper Liberi" (Mountaineers Are Always Free). A farmer stands to the right and a miner to the left of a large rock bearing the date of admission to the Union, June 20, 1863. In front of the rock are two hunters' rifles with a Phrygian cap, or a "cap of liberty," resting at the cross of the rifles.

It is unusual for a state to have more than one official song. West Virginia actually has several. The oldest and most popular, "The West Virginia Hills," with words by Ellen Ruddell King and music and chorus by Henry Everett Engle, was completed in 1885 in Gilmer County and designated an official state song in 1947.

To read the lyrics, visit this website:

**www.netstate.com/states/symb/song/wv_hills.htm**

# Glossary

**armory**    A place where weapons such as guns are stored; also called an arsenal.

**biotech**    Short for "biotechnology," the use of living organisms to make useful products.

**denomination**    A smaller set of people within a broader religious group that believes in the same traditions and practices.

**diverse**    Very different or showing a great deal of variety.

**ecologically**    Relating to the environment and the way that humans, plants, and animals live together and affect each other.

**feud**    A long, bitter disagreement or fight between two groups or families.

**gorge**    A narrow valley with steep, rocky walls, usually with a stream or river running through it.

**immigrants**    People who come from a foreign country to live permanently in another place.

**median age**    The age, in years, where half of the people in a group are younger and half are older than that age.

**paleontology**    The branch of science that deals with animal and plant fossils.

**plantations**    Very large farms or estates where crops are raised using laborers who live there.

**pollinate**    To transfer or carry pollen from one plant to another to allow fertilization. Plants need this to reproduce.

**salamanders**    Amphibians with a lizard-like appearance. Amphibians live in water and breathe through gills when young, then develop lungs and live on land as adults.

**tannic acid**    A yellowish-brown or reddish substance that comes from some bark or plants.

# More About West Virginia

## BOOKS

Gordon, Nick. *Coal Miner*. Dangerous Jobs. Minneapolis, MN: Torque Books, 2013.

Horn, Geoffrey. *John Brown: Putting Actions Above Words*. Voices for Freedom: Abolitionist Heroes. New York: Crabtree Publishing, 2010.

Somervill, Barbara A. *West Virginia*. From Sea to Shining Sea. Danbury, CT: Children's Press, 2009.

## WEBSITES

**Official West Virginia State Website**

www.wv.gov

**West Virginia Division of Tourism**

gotowv.com

**West Virginia Legislature's Page for Kids**

www.legis.state.wv.us/educational/kids_page/fun_facts.cfm

## ABOUT THE AUTHORS

**Rick Petreycik** has written several books in the It's My State! series and has been published in a variety of magazines. He lives in Connecticut with his wife and daughter.

**Gerry Boehme** was born in New York City, graduated from the Newhouse School at Syracuse University, and now lives on Long Island with his wife and two children. He is a published author and editor, a businessperson, and an international speaker.

# Index

Page numbers in **boldface** are illustrations. Entries in **boldface** are glossary terms.

# Index